Aeolian Harp
volume 8

Edited by Gloria Mindock & Ami Kaye

Guest Editor: Gloria Mindock
Series Editor: Ami Kaye
Project Manager: Royce Ellen Hamel
Layout, Book & Cover Design: Steven M. Asmussen
Cover Artist: Tracy McQueen

Fonts "National Oldstyle", "Persnickety", and "Metro Thin" designed by
Andrew Leman, courtesy of The H. P. Lovecraft Historical Society, www.cthulhulives.org

Aeolian Harp Series: Anthology of Poetry Folios
Volume 8, First Printing
Copyright © 2021 Glass Lyre Press, LLC
Paperback ISBN: 978-1-941783-88-7

All rights reserved: Except for the purpose of quoting brief passages for review, no part of this book may be reproduced or transmitted in any form or by any means, electronic or mechanical, including photocopying, recording, or by any information storage and retrieval system, without permission in writing from the publisher.

Glass Lyre Press, LLC
P.O. Box 2693
Glenview, IL 60025

www.GlassLyrePress.com

Foreword

Gloria Mindock, Guest Editor

There is so much happening in the world: the war in Ukraine, the pandemic, on top of what our own personal lives confront. To handle it all, we writers look to life around us as well as our own.

Full of distinct voices doing just that, this anthology is an eclectic volume of poetry that will hold its readers captive through emotion, imagery, word play, and beauty. Some writers write about their experiences, life events, family, while others intrigue us with their amazing play with language and form.

Each poem flows from beginning, to middle, and ends so naturally it could be made into a short film. Writer Nicole Greaves states, "I choose to create, which is my power." Each poet writes about things from their own perspective, with music that embraces the poem and unifies its stanzas. Poems, like fingers on a keyboard, play with us to bring out their unique melodies. Sharon Alexander, a poet included in this anthology, states, "The joy, for me, is when the poem sings, that moment when the poem takes on a life of its own."

So, yes, open this volume to be woven into the landscape. Let its poems bring you to a new place, singing.

...this harp which I wake now for thee
  Was a siren of old who sung under the sea.

— Thomas Moore, *The Origin of the Harp*

Folios

Sharon Alexander	1
Margo Berdeshevsky	9
Susan Michele Coronel	21
Marcene Gandolfo	31
Nicole Greaves	39
Raewyn Kraybill	49
Brad Rose	59
Lindsey Royce	69
Leslie M. Rupracht	79
Diana Woodcock	89

Sharon Alexander

It's challenging to discuss one's aesthetic approach to poetry without feeling it's a luxury given our particular time in history. I often feel if I'm not writing about the pandemic, the climate crisis and now the war in Ukraine, my poems might be irrelevant. I've heard many other writers express similar concerns. However, as Audre Lord so eloquently stated, "Poetry Is Not A Luxury". It's a necessity - especially now.

Whatever's going on around me filters through my work whether I'm aware of it or not. The important thing is that I don't silence myself, that I find a way to respond to the world as it continues spinning.

I approach poetry as an observer by paying attention and following what captures my imagination. I begin with an image, a sound, the feel of the wind, a fleeting scent, a memory from childhood. Once captivated by the sensation, image or memory, I become the field observer, allowing the words to develop over time; to reveal themselves to me.

I'm a poet of place. I'm obsessed with crows and ravens. I love the stark beauty of the desert. I'm a creature of the forest and the mountains. The sea is a constant element, like a chorus, in many of my poems as I've often lived near large bodies of water.

I'm also a poet of rhythm and sound. I write lyrics, prayers, birdsong, breath, breeze, waves, rain. Poetry is meant to be heard, to be read aloud - the music brings all the elements together.

Writing allows me to see through a wider lens. I experience grief, joy, beauty, rage, passion in such a way that it no longer belongs to me. This perspective of seeing a larger landscape leads me to a place of compassion.

The joy, for me, is when the poem sings, that moment when the poem takes on a life of its own. Then I invite you, the reader, in. It's my wish that the poem will take you somewhere you didn't expect to go.

Blood Season

my body
a ticking wire
anchored to the belly
of the world

all the circuits sing

all the blood tides rip
and every pulse
an hour gone
every breath
a year in flight

my hair was dark and long
I walked with lovers in sin and grace
my voice a river
carving time

and for a minute
I believed
the star-strewn sky
blinked at me

and for an hour
I believed
the blood season
was eternity

Insomnia

If you could, you would sleep in the arms of the mesquite

Desert wind rattles bony limbs

Splintered stars shatter night's shell

The moon drowns her shadow in a porcelain cup

At the well of Holy Water, you wash your red hair

Dip your hands, drink, your mouth stained with blood

At the crossroads you swallow the turquoise glow

Night kneels before you—

*****

Night kneels before you—

At the crossroads you swallow the turquoise glow

Dip your hands, drink, your mouth stained with blood

At the well of Holy Water, you wash your red hair

The moon drowns her shadow in a porcelain cup

Desert wind rattles bony limbs

Splintered stars shatter night's shell

If you could, you would sleep in the arms of the mesquite

A Procession of One

for Leonard Cohen

It's four in the morning in early November.
I stand in the shadows, my wristwatch is broken.

The light in your window flickers and dwindles,
your face through the glass, a still life of grace.

Daybreak arrives while I wait at your gate.
I hold in my hands a book of your poems,
a lock of your hair and a dozen white roses.

Now that you're leaving, clouds shroud the sun,
the roses are crushed and my raincoat is tattered.

The taxi you summoned waits at the curb—
your quiet departure a procession of one.

Reliquary

In the dark cabinet
my grandmother hides
her jewelry

Cossacks she cries

It repeats itself—
history—bloody
sidewalks, genocide

The Pogrom she cries

In my dreams
she wanders beneath the starless
Odessa sky

Holocaust she cries

Oven and ashes
gold teeth and bones
her mother father sister

In the dark
cabinet
my grandmother
hides

In the Half-Light of the Forest

The older I become, the more the landscape resembles me.
—*Charles Wright*

familiar trees lean in
I feel them peer at me
older than last year
with snow in my hair
my eyes a hazy sky
remembering
red cardinals in winter
summer's first fireflies
how words on the page
are another kind of birdsong
how the landscape hints at autumn
a show of copper leaves
the meadow laced with early frost
my shadow growing long.

They Cut You Open/The Crows Escape

Imagine the surgeon's surprise—a whoosh of wings
rhythmic beat, they soar out double doors
rise to meet winter clouds—
black-winged scalpels
slice the sky.

In the waiting room, a huddle of worry, we flock and hover.
Outside the window, a bare-branched tree sheathed
in ice. Shadows fall from frozen
limbs—another dark bird
takes flight.

Behind swinging doors that bright room echoes—
tools clatter, a whir of machinery. Nurses
aflutter in wing-tipped caps nod
and murmur. The room
slows, grows quiet.

Now the surgeon removes his gloves. Your body
still on the steel table—you rise. Alone
and weightless, you float above.
In the distance you hear
the rattle of crows.

Margo Berdeshevsky

Blessings are everywhere and so damn hard to believe in. Now it is our frighteningly violent spring 2022, when the smallest buds demand to open and to live another year, as we do. Here we stand. Here we write. Here we dare to make poems.

How to write poetry in war time, how to clean the ash out of the heart quickly enough to mix it with metaphor and the scent of an ending and another terrible beginning, or blood that is too near and too distant to admit to my/our own fear? And yet, word-presences come near me, spiritual, metaphorical, hard edged and soft—insisting that I include them somehow.

That's where my works come from in these times. I find that my poems may allow me to go where simple definition and description cannot. Or at least where I cannot without layering and overlaying my own words and images. Sometimes I'm dyslexic. Endings come before the middles or the starts, and I must reshape to find a true order. I begin to understand that this process is like some fraught attempt to find order in my universe. I try. I rewrite. Reorder. Find the shape that I can live with and say, there, that's said/ that's done, for now. And then, I must be silent and let the works speak, I hope, for themselves. I don't like to be a poet who "explains" her work. But to be honest, I have been feeling this year that my Cassandra hair is on fire. I know what I am afraid of. So do you, the reader, the thinker. And that is where we meet—each of us—in the empty space filling with our fears, imaginings, deaths, and lives.

May we make it through these days with a little grace, and a recognition that, as Lisel Mueller wrote in her poem, "The Blind Leading the Blind"

"Something with wings went crazy against my chest once.
There are two of us here. Touch me."

Between Tree and Rocket

*They don't distinguish between a tree and a
rocket, a human and a pile of stones*
 —*Mosab Abu Toha*—The Nation/ *May 2021*

When I stop at dusk's window
the raven is hunting in the sparrow's den
for her egg — food for his own nesting mate

The ovule falls   and breaks
the raven lifts — What was
a bird— is useless now to either.

Here night will rise as the super flower
blood ecliptic moon across its umbral
shadow of an earth, and dirt, and sun.

(Not noted— in a desert where the bombs
spin — where skin can be seen from
hiding— before it lands on stones.

Or one torn silk voice of neighbor
killing kin— Dust, once stones,
—moonlit across its land.)

Here, a neighbor died alone in her one
room— found after a few or eleven
days— natural causes, not murdered then,

another neighbor mouths.
Folding news into its used silk shroud
—Torn note without music. —

When I walk out from my
room—there's the torn old man
masturbating on the street,
exposed flesh covered in wrinkled dust.

Against my birthday night I fold
and open and fold
ones who are not
distinguished as tree or rocket or stone.

Only hungry
for milk — for birth—for a nesting stone—.
A neighbor who folded alone.

~

One Answer, Or None To Hers Or His Or Mine...

How you have painted the painter from
inside his star splattered mind and made
monologue of his almost sweet decline

how a home fire chokes
all in its path—not enough rain or
hope to save or doors to bar — how

sleet at last stilettos our winter
visions— a bitch high-heeled femme
determined to frighten Sunday dawn
into submissions minus sleep

how I ache to run naked in the painter's
calla lilies jonquils amber or
yours — you will say the painter made
them live—even so—even so

the rest of us are afraid of
our dying   of their dying-minute scorched
sky —grieving for more than breath or
door or paint or prayer will heal

who will paint a door in it, what saves
too vast   too old   too young
even so

how a star splattered mind
can hold a breath
if you draw it well enough

color knifing through—
if you whisper it in
terrible dark until wing-fall

There will be—
— a terrible bright

~

* With thanks to Lois P Jones for her inspiration

All Night. Please.

Once, I called her the darkness. Now, I call her
Eclipse-*me*. Half a sky-*me*. Child-*me*. Nipples hot with
mid-life,   night-lit,   me.

Where the dark of a pulsar shimmers
like a baby burning.

As though a soul were an egg, a breadfruit, a plum, so full, so
ripe, so ready to be injured by falling. But say I find faith. No.
Say a volcano's silver sword stabs my sleep. No. Say guardian.

Its charred descent, its white split-tailed birds, diving.
Say goddess of ash. Say ash of kiss. Say ebbing courage, even when
prayer and what is that?   has a star's clack of visible radiation.

Please   say I'm a good girl.   Still.

Say a spider's sticky gray threads are all the strings inside my skin
and that child I am wants to say thank you to someone,   still.
Infested heart   go away,   go home.   Fall.   Get out of my heart.

I will lie with the only lover left : sky.
Double ringed, led by its tiny chain across the sudden black
ecliptic,   and a golden ring to protect it. I've married my

self, now. Dressed me in my skimpy gown. Cleaned
inside my bones with steel brushes. Hid from dogs in the bed
while my own eclipse is a solarized star, crossed out by moon,

dropped down between my woman's sway and burden. There,
my hermit's candle, and nipples flamed.
Like all surfaces,   I can fracture.

No neutron-fast-percussions, imitating guardians of time.
No. Summer's first clean white nights will come — still — and still
— twice the darkness, heard.

Still, the child I am wants to say : thank you,
to someone, someone, please.
Say star. Say eclipse. Say I am a good child.
In the dark. All night. Still.
Please.

~

Bridge in the City of Light

Graffito in fluorescent green hisses on the lowest iron beam
under its arch facing the Notre Dame that burned   was it

only spring-times ago? did those then long spears of fire
touch or come from angels or hate or grief or is there now

a vaccine good for ire or memory or loss? how will I know.
Yesterday under that bridge across from Our Lady dressed in

her corset of scaffolding raised now for renewal   spring
blossoms insist now as then —nonetheless—

while a bright graffiti sprays its dark philosophy   will I cry
or cringe   not for one burned cathedral or faith that can be

rebuilt   not for any cross or any creed or any spring   but brilliant
under its hidden from sunshine arc   green letters blazed nonetheless

: *Je suis cet astre qui provoquera le plus beau désastre. Signed Yellow Star.*
(I am that star that shall provoke the most beautiful disaster. Signed Yellow Star.)

Was such a yellow star ever part of some other fire ? Or is it
too late or too soon to forget ?

Something dark   or something beautiful   scrawled
under a bridge in this later century of flames ?

Does something slouch this way again or again or
is there a scaffold still to hold a springtime

vine of light   its repetitious climb?   Not now —
or not later?   or   *what exactly is a beautiful disaster ?*

~

Postlude

Leaf fall dirt-caked as love half buried, its skeletal hands
that waved *come home* — infants in someone's embrace,

aged next — to shout how the personal was political, political
the personal before their winning hands were maimed —

land after land — note makeshift memorials strewn with
children's pens, stems of what were flowers, burned cauls.

It was journalists who were massacred that year,
that winter riot. Prelude to fascist boots on lost ground.

Lost ground. Then
we called it democracy. Then we called it America.

In the beginning was —a word— fine toothed as a soul—
hand-held — personal — political — gunned in its birth

zone. Kali Yuga they'll call it now on one side of the mount.
On this slope of dirt — in the beginning was the word we

wanted more   and the word was human.
No. Prelude. Leaf-fall.

* epitaph for a land in its lost days

Ripening

Dawn has no eagles no claws no butterflies, a soul-silence only monasteries and mountaintop holies had, before. But that was before and this is day at the end of beginning. There was only

going to be a beginning, once. You have started at the end to watch without eyes. To poem without voice. To wait for your flesh to be written by your own unmade bed. A heartbeat born

out of fear, and soothed by silence. Nothing is gifted but walls and grace and white space. How could it be grace, the blind eye insists and the wall holds its counsel. Your marriages

have not happened yet, not the first not the second not the third and the one in the dark — that person someone has informed you has died. You will learn to be sad. The lover has

not said "this was not a marriage" yet, and the rapist has not said "you can go now" yet, and the unrequited has always remained so. You are pure without knowing why. You are not clean

you are not dressed but you are not spoiled. You do not understand arithmetic or viral sciences. You are a swan-necked girl with large hips and a starvation for applause. A femme

in silk.   You are flame before it is stone.   You are walking toward you   Trembling with wish   Doe with no forest to hide you   Your blood cells already know there are no promises

What if no one touches you ever. There is no birth day no double helix no mother no father no messengers but your word is a name whispered in storm. Is a handprint on water. Is sprouted

from a vernal branch along with its single leaf.   You must learn to open. If this is meant to be a tree, what is a woman then.   Gather her into your own sleep, your body, ripening—

~

Susan Michele Coronel

Poetry is an important part of who I am and how I see the world. It helps me to understand and transform challenging life events, and to celebrate the magic and beauty of everyday experiences. It is also a way to tap into the subconscious mind, and to access a dormant imagination. I like poetry's specificity, its idiosyncrasy, and its mystery.

I draw on many sources in my work—direct experiences that I have felt, witnessed, and lived, as well as works of visual art, especially by female artists who are not widely known. To access surreal imagery, I allow myself time for more play and tinkering, and focus less on the intellect, meaning, and making sense. I am drawn to unexpected juxtapositions and welcome the opportunity for unrelated objects to dance and sing. I believe less is more, and through repeated revision, I pare down the poem to its essential core.

When I write ekphrastic poems such as the ones selected here, I impose on myself the structure of a time limit, and often refer to a list of random words. I follow the words and their associations, as well as the music of the language, to where they, and not necessarily I, want to go. Like Richard Hugo's triggering town, I trust that my subconscious will reveal the bigger, deeper subject to me. In my ekphrastic work, I explore the relationship between word and image to advance a feminist perspective on how gender and sexuality shape the gaze, eros, and the imagination.

Writing poetry is a richly rewarding path. There is always new subject matter to explore, and new art works in which I can immerse myself. I read voraciously, and I am always seeking opportunities to learn more about craft and new ways to access the imagination. For me, writing poetry is also not a solo pursuit. It involves exchanging works-in-progress with fellow poets, writing together using generative prompts and time limits, collaborating with other artists, and sharing poems with the community through such avenues as open mics and journal-sponsored readings.

SOMEONE'S IN THE KITCHEN

After the photograph "Women's Work—Housewives' Kitchen Apron" by Birgit Jürgenssen

I am a comely wife
yet I hallucinate
dust bunnies
soap powder & grease.
My membrane
is fluid — I scrawl
help and please
on my pristine apron
& on the walls
of the washing machine.
I want to topple
into an animal world.
Mark me
milk me
tape me
lock me
mock me
but don't burn
my freckled frock
when the iron's
too hot.
My ovaries sizzle
in the oven
like a blazing opera. I want
to lay hands on
my own damn freckled
throat, compel my
monstrous,
coal-fired mouth
to vocalize
every aroma
& tang.

NOT WALKING ON EGGSHELLS IN RIO DE JANIERO

After the photograph "Entrevidas" by Anna Maria Maiolino

The eggs are not aware of how I waltz
as I twist and turn around them like a capoiera dancer.

When I was six, Mrs. Bederman set up an incubator
in the classroom. I held the eggs against my chest,
shells still warm. When the chicks hatched, I let one
spring over my wrists, little feet indenting my palms.

I inhaled the scent of sawdust & popcorn, fluffy feathers
pulsing softly like a bulb, the chick so tiny and light,
I could have crushed it with a flinch of my hand.

Now I am marching barefoot around scattered eggs
on cobbled streets, navigating a minefield
of metaphors: fragility, disorder, hope of new life.

To avoid the brutality of smashing an egg
is an elaborate choreography. Do I swerve enough
to avoid complicity in violence?

Dictators don't understand metaphors.
The rest of us know how dangerous it is
to live even one day.

A PORTABLE PRISON

From a photo of Ketty La Rocca's performance, "La mie parole et tu [my words and you]"

My neighborhood was not designed
for this type of antagonism.
I avoid the tension of pointing hands
that emit nervous energy, transmitted
to my core by telephone & telepathy.
What's the best form of engagement
when the mind is like a portable prison?
No concentration on honest answers.
Instead, people sing plague & panic
under sordid skies, lose their fingertips
in hair as long slender stalks of calla lilies
droop from a vase's mouth.
You can take a mind anywhere,
like breath trapped inside a balloon.
I beseech it not to break.

A MUDDLED MIND

After the painting "A Muddled Mind That's Never Confined" by Jade Fadojutimi

knows the patchwork of puzzlegrass
& the hopeful swallow
of furry bodies ululating as they kiss
starburst-stained glass,
a shimmering fairytale
that doesn't believe in fairytales
but in its own self-worth

Sometimes I'm a spider with insomnia
scaling the walls
wet with pomegranate shimmer,
a freedom summer
of jaunty jukeboxes
& slipped discs

The furious burn of tomorrow
is sometimes too fast to contain,
bursts on the scene like exploding ink —
& don't forget the power
of the atomic clock —

time to get translucent
& shine a flashlight away from the past,
open my eyes,
allow the entry of fevered thoughts
like holy water dripping off the corners
of a linen washcloth
as it tints plums green
I might take out the trash
but leave it scattered
like scattergrass —

My muddled mind is never confined,
even as it dives into darkness & smiles,
muttering *I'm sorry, I'm not sorry*
like a smudged daydream

THE POWDERPUFF PRINCESS DOESN'T BELONG TO A WORLD OF CHROME AND KISSES

After the photo "Untitled, Florida" by Vivian Maier

because in a frosted fur stole she's alone and dazed in a parking lot, ditched after her boyfriend was toted away in a paddy wagon for bashing in a man's head so hard, the man bled bright shards. Stars blink at the Thunderbird, its chrome and upholstery anticipating rip and burn. The background sounds are doo-wop and drip. No mirror to confess, no glass slipper to caress, only the echo of high heels clacking the pavement in a swirling field of lampposts and neon signs. She cannot drive or adjust her beehive, just wipe salty tears on the back of her glove. She's a solitary swan in a grown gown running from the rhythm of the radio and her own blinking, the swish of passing cars spitting gravel on her ankles on this impossible Saturday night.

CALL ME STRIPED BUT NOT HIDDEN

After the painting "First Signs of Spring" by Inka Essenhigh

in the blur of what I am—
Remember the fox, moonlit.
A canopy of tentacled trees

pantomimes the part of mothers,
mothers who shame, mothers
with glazed eyes & tears

of cool, vaporous mint,
mothers evading pre-dawn delusions.
I am tenderly tonguing the inside

of my cheek, tangled in long skeins
of fluorescent pink yarn
that entwines all daughters.

What is the etymology
of knot and coil? What happens
when roots & branches

begin tasseling, intent to unravel
the muse maker's magnetic molecules,
the lodestar of lift & burn?

Marcene Gandolfo

When I surrender to the poem, to its language, its music, its images, I let the poem take me to a new place, even if that place feels frightening and uncomfortable. I find the poem often knows more than my linear, conscious mind can express, so when I write, I trust the poem, allow it to lead me, surprise me, teach me more about myself and my relationships in this world. These poems reflect my ongoing meditations on girlhood, motherhood, connection, and alienation.

Cleave

Yes. It's true. It isn't supposed to happen this way. A girl opens her curtain to a deepening orchard. And yes. She runs through. She runs in spite of mother. She runs until she's shadow. She runs until her name is a thumbprint on mother's coffee cup. And each night she runs over mother's skin, light and quick and spidery until mother shudders and wakes and every morning is February. In an empty theatre the girl recites her letters. She addresses them mother. In a hollow mailbox mother opens and closes her afternoon. The girl runs over mother's morning papers and breakfast toast and the fruit that tastes like fruit from a deepening orchard. The girl runs for miles around prayer chains and ribbons and wishing wells. She runs until no orchard lives behind the curtain. Until mother is not a mother anymore. Until no fruit grows over the road to the home that turns to shadow. In an empty theatre the girl recites her letters. She addresses them mother.

When She Leaves, I Think of Demeter in Autumn

I forget the taste of blood
from a velvet peach,

the bruised season's
last hours.

Now she's just a sun's
afterimage.

At first I thought I'd lost
my own body,

felt it slip with the wind.
Then I began

to practice the faith
of bare trees,

learned to enter winter,
an empty cathedral,

enter nights as dreams
that sing

in different shades
of green.

Exit

In the season of unspeaking,
after days of closing whispers,
the unwelcome yellow August,
ivy hours, dimming sonatas,
weeks of suitcases that clasp
in the key of B-flat, his hands,
those holy whispers, leave
the unanswered house that asks.

Once

I felt the devil's cloak
violent hot—
made from the red coils
of my mother's stove.

I never wanted to touch
the devil but the other
choirgirls told me it was sin
to pray to Mary

to keep my rosy prayer beads
I wanted to be a good
choirgirl with perfect pitch
then I missed a note.

I could smell my burnt flesh
taste the scorched finger
in my mouth it was better
than the taste of nothing.

Circle with Two Lines from Job

When my mother broke the gold-veined mirror
we knew what it meant

though she wouldn't let me speak it, *Seven years
bad luck,* seven years.

We drew open the curtain, kissed the shadows
that led us through a mist

which made us shiver. For years glass
resounded, a broken clock chime

striking, but then my body felt a fever
breaking, triumphant sweat

at the temple. The priests taught us to sing,
Who can discover

*the face of his garment? Who can open
the doors of his face?*

We chanted our way to a labyrinth. At last
a gate opened

to a field of ripe wheat. I knew it would lead us
back to where we began.

Today my mother kneels down, lays her ear
against the cracked earth

and says she hears singing.

Lorca's Guitar

You say a scar is just a line of music, written to skin, a string of notes, a row of old shirts that trembles a clothesline. Last night, I traced my scar in the cold light, as I rose from a hot bath that turned tepid. I remembered how my infant daughter loved water until she listened to the pull of the drain. I guess we all cry in the fear of disappearing. I'd towel her wet body, rock her against my chest until I'd hear her exhale. Tonight she sings in a distant city, strums a gypsy guitar. I miss her music when the teakettle's shrill cuts winter air. Tonight my old scar rests inside a soft robe, by a warm teacup, near a fireplace, where the last kindling collapses to ash. Even the dying fire keeps my feet warm. Tonight I let the scar exhale.

Nicole Greaves

I wrote recently about my early love of words and memories of my mother reading to me, speaking primarily in English, in her meaty accent, but sometimes in Spanish. Language connected us, and when she spoke to her sister in Spanish, it could also divide us since I was not proficient in her native tongue. Language, as we know, has power, and its greatest power is to teach, to help us understand our human experience.

Poems help to chart time. They are logs I write, as if I were on a voyage, to orient myself in the elements, understand velocity, and reflect. Poems can come at me like the wind. Ruth Stone talked about poems traveling this way. This is inspiration, and sometimes it is like this, Plato's "mania." I love when this happens, and I wish this was always the case. When it does happen, poems can slip away from you, as noted in "My Father Poem"; if you cannot write them down, you often lose them. In my busy, fragmented life, this occurs a lot. Sometimes poems are slower to come. I hear clips of one, as if it were behind a door, muttering to itself. I assemble it, piece by piece. At times, poems focus on a moment in the way a telescope does a place. Other times, they explore the arc of many journeys. Or they speak through or to an other. The best poems zoom in and are also panoramic. They move from the feeling of sand under a fingernail to the horror of another missing young woman. They connect the ordinary and the sublime. Poetry in its newness hearkens to what is ancient, living both on our lips and in our neurons. My mentor Lucie Brock-Broido told me that poetry is like a tree; the trunk, the heart of the poem as the branches push out into the world while always returning toward that heart. I tell my students this, and that poetry is us alive with our senses.

My book, *Having Witnessed the Illusion*, focuses on childhood as the daughter of an immigrant, becoming a mother, and my mother's death. The poems in this folio were born closer in time. In this case, my journey was turning fifty and entering the pandemic as my children finished and started college. There were so many things that were beyond my control, beyond any of our control. I thought of my pregnant mother standing on a street corner, left by my father to build a life for her and her child. My pregnant, social worker mom. In this state, she chose to observe the beauty of the world and to repair the damage or hold it close when she couldn't. Beauty, restoration, and devotion are three things I try to show in my work. I choose to create, which is my power.

The Cardinal

Each year he comes back
like a hand flying out of a dream,

brighter than I remember
as if he spent the winter in

someone's mouth. Some say he is
the dead coming to remember us.

How is that he survives
like a heart beating in a tree?

He sings to his beloved
through bad weather, though we

never see her. We should
welcome him back, set out

feeders, but we don't,
yet he stays for the summer.

I Turn Fifty a Month
before the Pandemic

The overture has a life of its own, the announcer
said this morning, *no one remembers the opera.*

Two ancient nuns repeat this as they walk
hand-in-hand in teal coats, through the morning fog.

Write this down, one says, *we must remember.* I had
relinquished all hope that the day might matter, that there

could be something, then I heard whistling
through a blue door, then this. You are always

twelve and twenty-two, with each promise, even when
you start to lose things. A flood of warmth envelops me,

like being born a girl. I continue after the sisters, close
enough to overhear, as if I were a tiny cloud above them.

A Year Without Snow

My neighbor shoots off a gun to ward
the virus off. *It can't hurt. It's better*

than the evil eye. I crack a smile
in the shape of the stale fortune cookie

I had for lunch when I thought about
how I used to believe that my mouth was

dramatically large, until my new dentist told
me *it's teeny-weeny, almost nonexistent,*

but no one I told believed this. I persisted.
She said, *It's canary small.* Today, I found

two fortunes, like two yokes, identical
for emphasis: *Relearn everything*

you are. At thirteen, I'd have scotch-taped
that across my locker so that it was shiny

like tempera. Along with, *You have to forgive*
yourself. Now I just hang wind chimes.

My neighbor asks: *Do you care?* I shrug as he
lets off another shot. We're all breaking down

a little. The gunfire smells like Christmas,
and I'm caught between looking back

and ahead. My feet are ridiculously cold,
as if I were standing barefoot in snow.

In from the Rain

What is lived through becomes the dark air
in the circumference of singing bowls distilled by light,

all the imperfections as visible as my tobacco skin,
the mariachi band panting between sessions

when the bowls are struck, a lullaby between courtships
without a dollar to spare for an offering.

Somehow someone still calls me
Sweetie before he really sees my face, how old I am,

and I remember it: a smile like an envelope
opened with greasy fingers in a hot kitchen.

Then there is just the embarrassment of being
mistaken. That carelessness of desire.

The soup comes out steaming with recovery.
The metals of the trumpet begin again,

the bowls and chintz around me catch the light
and spark like summer, how I have come to think of it.

A Rubric for Their Suffering

When my children were small, I'd ask like the nurse:
"On a scale of one to ten, what is the level of your pain?"

Or what is the need measured in hugs,
or, sometimes, jelly beans. "No, not a 100.

Something reasonable." We must learn to regulate,
despite the contradictions. It's more complex now:

this rubric. "How close are you to the fire?
From walking into the sea?" *Assembling a strategy,*

one might respond and the other, *Exceeding expectations.*
"Can you open the window? Is there a lifeboat nearby?"

The window is painted shut, but I have a hammer, one says.
The other, *Only a tire.* "What else? What else?"

I can climb out on the fire escape, throw confetti.
I can draw a perfect sun and eat a salami sandwich.

It'll have to do. I have to stay up with Dostoevsky
and the dusky sky like in a Whistler painting.

In high school, my son had a teacher with a sign
taped to her desk that read: In Life There are No Make-up Tests.

It was peeling at the edges. On conference days,
I peeled a little more, like at a scab. The teacher practiced law,

but gave it all up for them. *It had to be a calling.*
My daughter calls home in the middle of the night

in her first month of college when a hallmate overdoses.
They're in lockdown. *Is everything ok?* she asks

the policeman, poking her head out of her door, like a mother
herself. "No, it's not. Get back in your room. This is not

for you to see." *Which one is it? The boy whose shoes
are too big so that he looks like he is always*

walking through puddles? She wonders. He can't come
back, no second chance. His mouth like coal

hardened with a million years of light. From the window,
she watches him hoisted into a darkness, sealed in

a bag like laundry. The police knock on the doors,
say, "Don't go it alone." Another one is crying.

Maybe he was the one who had prepared for this,
who pressed his mouth against the boy's

with all his weight, like saving his own brother.
"How are you feeling?" I ask. She says, *Like never before.*

My Father Poem

When my father was dying, I didn't go to see him.
Instead, I sent him gardenias, open infant palms
pulsing over their first surprise.

It was my mother's favorite scent, which she wore
in excess, the replica she could manage of her
girlhood home in the Panamanian countryside

where she said there was always an ideal moment
between when things ripened and decayed. I image
this ideal like those perfect words that describe

what sits inside you as jewels that come
when you can't write them down, like in the self-check-
out at the grocery store. My father left her pregnant

with me in her fifth month on a street corner,
with fifty dollars. He wasn't ready. It wasn't his fault.
My twenty-five-year-old mother, not quite five-two, was

showing by then, enough for people to start opening
doors for her as they do. She said it was an "exemplary"
(she liked that word) fall day in Boston, the leaves

in a shift from yellow to red that is orange but not quite.
It made her hopeful as beauty does, just as it
can make you feel vanquished. My mother died

a few years before my father from the same rare
cancer. It was just the beginning of spring.
My father died in Florida, so it didn't matter

what season it was, but it was spring too. I wanted
to send something. Be a good daughter. I wanted
his last breaths to be complete with her.

Raewyn Kraybill

I wavered between two dream jobs as a child, an environmental scientist and an author. Although I have chosen the path of a writer, I still love nature. This comes through in my poems, almost every one connecting back to and referencing nature. "I am the fig" came to life after I learned about the intriguing relationship between figs and wasps and I knew I had to write about it. My friend Benji Keeler helped me edit the poem "The Maldives are being swallowed by the sea. Can they adapt?" I pulled its title from an article about the natural disaster being caused by global warming in the Maldives. Nature is huge and dramatic, so what better to use to convey big emotions? I think nature is inherently poetic, and I love to work it into poems.

I'm a big fan of enjambment, especially the use of enjambment to give a line multiple meanings. If you read the line as just the line, not in the context of the enjambed sentence, it has an additional sentiment. I have experimented with a variety of organizations and forms, but I use free verse and one stanza a majority of the time.

My poetry can come off as very direct. I use a lot of second person, addressing or accusing the other or the whole world with my subject matter. I am a prose writer too, but unlike I do in prose, I don't soft-pedal anything. My lines are solid, bold statements. It's all about emotion and reflection. I think poetry is the form that it is easiest to fully stand behind what I think and feel. In writing my poems I often go back and delete words that try to mute the meaning. I write in absolutes. This is a voice throughout all my poems, a definitive, confident one.

The Maldives are being swallowed by the sea. Can they adapt?

Headline and quote from article by Tristan Mconnell

I am collapsing in on myself—
The Maldives are being swallowed by the sea. Can they adapt?
"We may lose who we are before we lose where we are."
It's good to be where you are.
It's too good. You passed me in your
car yesterday and even though I was the one in the headlights,
you were the deer.
It made me so sad I want to throw up. Like
in movies when they run down a hill and double over, but I
can't even cry so that's asking a lot.
I am collapsing in on myself—
I am in sadness so deep I can't get to the bottom of it.
And I know you never felt anything
like this for me, which is the hardest thing to understand.
I could never really hate someone that I didn't once love,
and when I read something I really liked I wanted to show it to you.
I hate you, but
I never wanted to hate the way you smell.
I am collapsing in on myself—
The Maldives are being swallowed by the sea. I don't think they can adapt. I'm sorry.

SCABS AND WALLPAPER

Just tell me something true
 and I'm yours.
Tell me about the way a knife feels digging into your skin.
Don't soften the pain with metaphors and flowery language.
Tell me the way it really feels.
Then tell me how you really feel
and I'll tell you if it hurts more than that knife.
I will peel the wallpaper off walls
and skin from my body until
I find something raw.
You know it's true.
I'm always picking at something.
I always want answers and never a question.
But you help me bandage my scabs
and I try to live knowing nothing much at all.

ATROCITY

I am realizing I'm in love with you on a rainy September night
You are making me tea- I don't know this yet
but I will commit the atrocity of falling out of love with you
I didn't want to- I will heal
in the place I was hurt and all alone
Seven months later
it is the last day- My love decays
with a long half life
I sleep and the Moon watches
The Earth will spin off its axis
In order achieve the briefly unimaginable
I turn my face towards the Sun- I squint
I wake to the feeling almost imperceptible
Not drowning anymore but now an empty bottle
The Ocean can swallow the land
like chasms and like hell
yet it can never wash away what you did to me.
But that part comes after
I don't know this yet- You are making me tea
I am realizing I'm in love with you on a rainy September night

I AM THE FIG

A wasp seeks shelter / She tunnels into a fig / Into the womb of the fruit she dies /
Leaves behind the pollen stuck to her / And proteins that made up her body

What even is it to die when you're a wasp / Instead / She dissolves / Becomes part of something else / A fig / Nourished by her corpse

It resides in a stand with dozens of other burial site fruits / Where I buy it and carry it around like a grudge / I hope when I bite into it I can taste the wasp / I hope she left a mark

It is an intricate ritual of an unlikely couple / The fig needs the wasp / The wasp takes comfort in the fig / But it would live just as well without it / And I am the fig / Always

HADES'S MONTHS

I stand on top of a
Pseudo greek building
Fifth ave is directly below me
So I don't look down on it as a god
But I do look down on it

Across the street someone waits at a bus stop
Like Persphone waits
to cross the Styx twice a year
I wonder how they see me
I see myself through their eyes
A figure standing alone in the dark
In the snow staring down at the street

The bus pulls up below me so close
I could step onto it if I had a more
Dynamic death wish
I imagine Hades taking my hand and
Helping me safely step onto it
Counting on that I would soon fly off the top
And hit the ground

But I don't step on it. I watch the person
Illuminated orange by the streetlights
Get on the bus. It sounds like a plane
Taking off. I climb down off the top of
This abandoned fountain building. I walk
myself home. I wonder if the
sinkholes lead to the underworld.
If they do, there are entrances all over.

In Pittsburgh it snows all winter. I thank
Persphone and her three pomegranate seeds
For this. I am content. I don't feel alone when

The snow is around. Snow may be ice crystals
But it is the warmest form of precipitation.
It insulates. It hugs.

I believe that Persphone sends
Snow to save the plants from the chill while
She is away. Everyone I see out with me now
I take communion with. Cold shortens the distance
Between two people.

Hades brings the dark
And the cold and the hard death of winter. Persphone
Sends snow to soften the ground and save what
Can be saved.
In Hades' months of the agreement
Hades kills what must be killed.
Persphone saves what can be saved.

River

There is a river running through my veins
And a smooth stone at my core
that has never been shaken
The eye of the storm
When I was born there was a hunk of rough stone there
and every time my heart raced it has smoothed over more and more
Rounded by the waves
When your heart beats really fast in the dark
you can feel that there is not blood pumping but really waves
and feel your body be washed over by them
The blood is just waves and can't you feel it wash through you
The ocean does not live in the conch shell
you raise to your ear it lives inside you
The rush of blood is the sound of the ocean
And what am I but a river
a bit of the ocean running another course
and so I can never drown
Life is just the casually relentless ocean
inside you and the rocks that it must smooth over
and the jaggedness that leaves in humans
because we are flesh and not only water
Water supports all life but I need it more than most
I need not to just consume it but to commune with it
and as I watch it I can wrap my hands around that
smooth stone and be still

Brad Rose

In these poems, as with much of my work, I'm concerned with word play, defamiliarization, the juxtaposition of unlikely associations, and dark humor. I write prose poems because, about 8 years ago, I began to feel that I had reached the end of what I felt I could accomplish with the lyric, predominately confessional poem. Instead, I wanted to experiment with a form that doesn't depend upon my own feelings and experiences, but is based on those of another (imaginary) person's. I wanted to employ a form that feels more congenial to humor and a third-person perspective (persona poem). I like the appearance of the block paragraph as it tries to contain the disorder and chaos of the speakers in many of my poems. (In "The Art of the Prose Poem (1999)" Russel Edson observes, "My ideal prose poem is a small, complete work, utterly logical within its own madness.") I also prefer the sentence to the line—as the poetic unit of measure. I think prose poems are more approachable, more "democratic" than lineated, lyric poems, because of their ease of reading. Even people who aren't interested in poetry can easily read a prose poem. When writing, I try to follow three precepts: 1) "Every view of things that is not strange is false,"—Paul Valéry, 2) "The function of the imagination is not to make strange things settled, so much as to make settled things strange."—GK Chesterton, and 3) "The ugly may be beautiful, but the pretty, never."—Paul Gauguin.

Cotton-Candy Pink

At the laundromat, I can hold my breath for half-an-hour. I don't know where one thought ends and another begins. Felicia has different colored wigs. One is cotton-candy pink. Once, she took me dancing. It was my birthday. The music was everywhere, but I noticed my thoughts were accelerating like it was too late. Some of them were talking in a secret language. Sometimes thoughts are like other people. They have their lives, while I'm having mine. No big deal. At the dance, it was a nice cross-section of people. They were all wearing clothes and shoes. Felicia said, *Ray, you look sad as a mall Santa*. I told her I like to dance, but I had some things I needed to do. A Sly and the Family Stone tribute band was taking everybody higher, so I went outside. In the dark, the city crouched down, and the buildings looked like a crowd of appliances. It was hot and I heard sirens in the distance. I wondered what was going on in the sky. They say when you sleep your muscles become paralyzed to stop you from acting out your dreams. I wanted to go back inside to dance, but the stars seemed lost, like they were moving to somewhere new and needed someone to say farewell. Felicia came outside to smoke a cigarette, and she said, *Oh, here you are*, like I was a surprise. Tonight, she wore a flame red wig. There were a lot of things I could have said when her two sleeping kids died in that Christmas blaze, but I didn't. I'm still not sure what color her real hair is.

Like an Accident

Saturday night, I drove out of town, into the desert, so I could count lightning strikes. Like a black balloon splattered with streaks of white paint, the sky stretched and spread until it popped. A couple of forks struck pretty close. On the way back, I stopped at *Cannibal's* for a drink. I love it when I order a Bloody Mary there. Nobody bats an eye. Charlene was there, drinking alone, so I told her about the time they wouldn't let me take my emotional support gator on the plane. She laughed so hard she nearly dropped her darts. *It's the damn government,* she said, as she recovered and hit the bullseye. I said, *Yeah, they're everywhere, but what are you going to do?* I like Charlene. Not sure whether her 4th husband just died or not. I don't think she's available, yet. If I had a life insurance policy, I'd let it expire. Never liked my next of kin. No sense of humor. Of course, thinking about the end is something everybody should do. It's perfectly natural. When my time comes, I'm going to make it look like an accident.

Suburban Landscape
(with Flying Saucer)

In the Great Big Picture Book of Lies my picture doesn't look like me. Recovering from a Lego injury, I'm wearing my mild socks. Mine is not a smile, but a simper. I'm not pushing the envelope, I'm an actor played by a husband. Sure, the kids are sober and the chimney has stopped smoking, but I look like an estranged taxidermist working remotely from a rental doomsday bunker in the Catskills. Clarise is mad at me, as usual. The car won't start. The house plants have died on my watch. The cat, emulating the parrot, imitating the dog, has begun barking. Sitting in the back yard now, as far away from the unpaid bills as is humanly possible to be and still reside at this address, I'm wondering if Michelangelo had had a dog, would he, Michelangelo, that is, have painted the Sistine Chapel or settled for linoleum? I have a life-long student debt, whose associated student escapades have placed me on the fast-track, in slow motion. I think we have termites. At night I can hear them chewing. The roof leaks when it's not raining. The washing machine refuses to rinse. Last week, I heard about a UFO crash on the edge of town. The mayor assures us it's nothing serious, but what does he know about interstellar debris? There are no signs of intelligent life in his administration. The museum closed, the schools are sub-par, the sub-flooring is optimal, and the overhead is killing me. Yesterday, when Jack came over, I hardly recognized his car, it was so clean. Ours is a moon vehicle covered in both brown dust and red rust—the earthy colors of an alien planet. Janine wants horseback riding lessons. She thinks *Equestrian* will look good on her college applications. Her sister is studying internet dating. I hate the neighbors, except for Michelle, the cute one, hemmed in on our cul de sac. She smiles at me like I'm not married. If I were to be fired from my current management-manqué job, it would be a celebratory disaster. I'm reading about how to become a change agent in a cashless economy. I'm afraid I'm coming up short. My pajamas are floral hectogons in a brilliant shade of jungle puce. When I drink, I see wires. I'm dieting exclusively on chocolate cake. Yes, we have roses growing along our white picket fence, but I don't understand the transmigration of souls. When the police arrive at our front door, I assure them I was nowhere near the scene of the crash, but inform them that ever since, Clarise has been acting a little funny. With his tentacle-like hand on his holstered firearm, the younger cop—the one whose face is slightly inhuman—tells me to put my hands over my head and that he knows the name of a good lawyer. It's his brother. He's new in town, he tells me, and doesn't yet have any reputation, to speak of.

Windows

Wednesday, on the way to the carwash, my car caught fire. And not the good kind, either. Sheila came running up to me and said, *Everything is getting worse and worse.* I told her the main problem is there's no solution. Everything has a life of its own. You keep trying and trying, but no matter how hard you try, before anyone knows you're gone, you're back where you started. Say, what ever happened to What's-His-Name? You know, Mr. It's-on-the-Tip-of-My-Tongue? Yeah, that guy; the one who hardwired the software and debugged the earworms. Before he disappeared, didn't he buy that bogus kidnapping and ransom insurance? I guess these days you can't be too careful. No, don't pay any attention to the venom-colored sunlight. I just painted the windows. They only look like they're snakes.

It All Depends

Admiring the corporeality of animals, we're parked in the ghost car. I have an indoor question: How many misspelled thoughts must I have, anyway? There's nothing more beautiful than wanting the impossible to be true, especially when it is. Time passes faster in the mountains, than it does by the sea. Like a drowned body, the sky's blue prairie floats overhead. Wind light as confetti. Maybe we should take a drive to the beach; go for a swim? I don't want to give away the ending, but I can tell you it's a beauty. No one attends their own funeral. Know what I'm saying? By the way, that outfit looks good on you. Although, it all depends on how you look at it.

Long Black Car

This time of year, the words on everyone's lips are, *No, no, not now.* Speaking of the dead; they come from a long, venerable line. But who's counting? Not even the mathematicians. A similar method is used in slaughterhouses. I'll spare you the details. My advice to you, *Stay focused. One size fits all.* Although many quantum theorists say we should abandon any notion of cause and effect, nothing succeeds like success. Discreetly, I whisper to Mr. Ruby, *Pull up the hearse.* And wouldn't you know it? Just like that.

Lindsey Royce

Primarily, what I strive for in art is a balance of emotion, wisdom, image, and sound. I inspire to impact my reader the way Dickenson describes in her 1870 letter to Thomas Wentworth Higginson: *"If I read a book [and] it makes my whole body so cold no fire can ever warm me, I know that is poetry. If I feel physically as if the top of my head were taken off, I know that is poetry. These are the only ways I know it. Is there any other way?"* I can't say I achieve that with any consistency, but that is my goal in writing poems—and sometimes we all hit that sweet spot. That said, I try write poems of a quality that transcends those folks who would (and have) distained my poems as confessional rubbish. Such criticism for a young writer is damaging. We poets are fortunate people: We have the truth of our lives from which to draw. We get to share our experiences, thoughts, spiritual insights, and feelings—so that we may connect with one another more fully and achieve the ultimate: to meet one another nakedly and fearlessly in that field Rumi names in the following poem translated by Coleman Barks. Here we see the mystery of writing poems as well as the idea of the use of metaphor when denotative language fails. Also, Rumi presses us to be awake to our world and every person, something that improves our lives, even when it hurts, like being present to the war in the Ukraine.

> "Out beyond ideas of wrongdoing and rightdoing,
> there is a field. I'll meet you there.
> When the soul lies down in that grass,
> the world is too full to talk about.
> Ideas, language, even the phrase "each other"
> doesn't make any sense.
> The breeze at dawn has secrets to tell you.
> Don't go back to sleep.
> You must ask for what you really want.
> Don't go back to sleep.
> People are going back and forth across the doorsill
> where the two worlds touch.
> The door is round and open.
> Don't go back to sleep."

What more could a poet hope for than to move a reader to a new awareness? I seek to do that in my poems.

The Connotation of Spells

I've been carrying a vial of black salt
in a suede pouch, talisman for protection,

gesture of love for mystery. Who has triumphed
over the unknown, erased her ache easily

as an amen swept from the prayerful lips.
The unknown sounds like a bell

but belongs to no one, not even the bell.
Maybe I'm becoming a white witch. I weave

and knit and make meaning with my altars,
each time new charms glisten there.

My belief is in my hands, strong and delicate,
that juggle seasons whole like sacred stones—

Himalayan Sea salt, moss agate, purple
fluorite, rough emerald. My small cauldron glows,

burning resins of copal, lavender, and
rosemary—meanings made as randomly

as those for tv love. My husband's death left
a phantom procession through my chest,

a path to his new history. I want to share in
the story he's writing on his side of the veil.

I want to fill my hollows with tender spells,
the fragrance of incense, the belly of song.

Tlazolteotl Comes to Me After The Ghost D&C

Tlazolteotl is the Aztec Goddess of purification, midwives, filth, and a patroness of adulterers. She a purification goddess, who forgives the sins and disease of those caused by misdeeds, particularly sexual misdeeds. She eats filth and gives birth to harmony and community.

My body starved sterile—first Robert's girl, then
Doug's boy—cells I could never hold long. Today, I'm
obsessed with the ghosts of beloveds—my newly dead
spouse, my best friend, my mom—left me
scorched as a mortar attack's third-degree burns,
with faith in an otherworld as a last resort.

Spirit is finally different than the Catholics I grew up with,
the priest, God's representative on earth,
who molested me, forced me to swallow his perversion.
I summon the dead with tinctures, and we talk,
sometimes over a drink, sometimes
I'm sobbing and begging for help. My never-babies

must've known, that broken, I would've wounded them, too.
They escaped me into the toilet bowl's baptismal waters
where they suffered the sewer to avoid me
as their mom. Stillborn, I'd have given them
a proper white-coffin burial. Please forgive me Kira,

please forgive me, Jayson. I never could have the D&C,
allowed you to leave at your pace. Did you ever leave me?
After the priest would molest me, I'd spit
into the toilet bowl, renew my power—

starvation, a mistake I would have taken a D&C
to unsuffer the shame and loneliness
the priest bred in me, to scrub my mind of his words
You'll never find a boy who'll treat you better than I do.

Today, unstarved and thick in body, I burn Palo Santo
smudge and Opopanax gum to cleanse his curse
as well as my anorexic thinking: I practice incantations,
my prayers dissolving with smoke, beseeching Tlazolteotl,

blessed Goddess of Filth, *eat my shame,* Tlazolteotl,
Goddess of Filth, *eat my self-loathing.* Tlazolteotl, Goddess
of Filth, *eat my belief, callous-stubborn, that fat and damaged,
I don't deserve love.* Tlazolteotl, from that filth, birth back
the woman I can be—mother me please so I can mother myself.

Mother Moon

Mother Moon is one of the trifectas of moon goddesses:
maiden moon, mother moon, and crone moon.
Mother Moon is depicted as pregnant.

When I had nothing, when baby, Kira, slid into the toilet bowl,
no proper white-coffin burial for her, I swallowed helplessness
in smooth pills. I held the open mouths of the bottles, those
pink and yellow O's slithered into my stomach. I greeted
them as a group, an audience of O's who slid easily into
their seats for a concert of O. There would be no baby, O,
there would never be a baby. Paramedics forced an O
down my throat, as I passed out wanting to get into the moon's
empty O. Instead, I vomited O's, every one, and woke
in a room loud with chrome and fluorescence, my Teflon womb
had unclenched Kira, I could not hold her in that unfaithful O.
The puke hose empty, the pill bottles empty, my womb four-
months filled, then empty with wasted menstrual blood, blood
moon red, I hardened, hollow and unfeeling. I even rejected
my cramps' sore O's. But I begged you, Mother Moon,
and your answer was that I would never be a mom,
and my heart turned to steel. My womb forever damaged,
birthed only pain. The O I groaned reached my mother
who didn't visit but loved with money, sent hundred-dollar bills
to the O of the moon's tip jar. I was sitting home alone, alone
with my hopeless O's, playing guitar, singing the saddest song
of howls, rocking with moans, O's inhuman and rising
from my animal body, all of me empty, even my dumbfounded
mind. The docs said I was lucky, I didn't care. I had slipped
into the heartless moon and was curled there, stunned at its bottom.
I was in the ruins of sun, that trickster, who shone brightly
the light of my failing. Tell me, how do you come back from that?

By the Roots

It was as if God raped me. The priest's desires
burrowed deep, became my secret . At seven, I hated

Catholicism for its sexism: girls wore white—gloves and veils
and carried rosaries, while boys had only to tuck shirttails.

And the priest in his purple robe consecrated sacraments
with his back to the congregation, as if he couldn't bear to see

me, his shame, shame that stole my hopes for heaven
and seared my spine upright with papal consent. Years later,

the Buddhist conundrum of emptiness pleased me; he had lain
dormant for years until humiliation swallowed me like Jonas and the whale

Now, I practice Buddhism and white witchery: male gods junior
to goddesses and sacred stones. When I light chakra candles,

orange to purge him from my womb and red to yank him
out by the roots, all the goddesses come to me at once,

those murdered women burned on stakes; be they Catholic saints
or Salem witches—all flesh smells the same when charred.

I seek to cleanse his perversion from my body, weeds
that have lived too long in my garden, have choked growth dead.

And watchful as an owl, and resolute as a fire siren—*the burning,
the burning*—I open my body with ritual, console the girl afraid to love.

An Ancestry of Roses

Rain that fell not an hour past
poured forever ago, though you can't
cut the rain like an ancestry of roses.
Go back beyond my mom to my
grand-mom to my great-grand.
You will find surnames dropped
like lit matches, flames doused on
wet asphalt. Our women set
remarkable luncheons: soups, fruit,
charcuterie plates with cheeses,
meats, nuts, and jams. Their napkins
were in rings, or if they felt festive,
folded into swans. The tables dressed
with French bone china shone three crystal
vases with their prized roses: yellow,
pink, red—and those Peace Roses
that looked to me like sherbet. The sun
that streaks the sky honey gold
is the same sun that rose forever ago.
Shears clipped over mounds of mulch
helped fists of buds grow open-
handed. Women, ripe with possibility,
tightened to seeds of bliss and ache
when their satin gowns trailed over thresholds.
A little spark of joy—the sharp shards,
the smooth, the mosaic manifests, generational.
I am the first daughter to howl down clothespins
and dust-rags, the first to daughter to eat food
with bare hands, save some sweet
for later. I am the first daughter unwilling
to fold my dreams for a man. I am a witch
who burns resins and casts white spells
instead of obeying a priest. I am destruction,
charring roses curled fetal in my path.
I am creation, making myth from sound,
image, space. I call for rain, for sun, for stars—
and what I call for is mine.

The Fool

I drew the Fool card that told me naivete is
shatterproof. A baby robin adorned the card's

face, beak parted, and I knew it was my throat
open to song. How often is inexperience kindling

for an immolation? How often is it a cairn
to mark a summit reached by dust-sweet sweat?

The fern behind the robin unfurls its fronds,
leafstalk then blade, and we call the leaf whole.

The Fool bears the number zero, before number
one and its competition, before multiples of grief--

abacus beads of origin. The O is not hollow but
a spoonful of kindness, a blue river stone

thrown into deep water. I'll risk being full
of emptiness, a fool heedless as a dandelion

poking through spring snow, dumb as a potato,
and, O, enlightened as its maker.

Leslie M. Rupracht

Daughter of artists and art teachers, I cherished early encouragement from my mother/muse and father/mentor. At five, I eagerly learned from Dad to operate film cameras, capture observations. At ten, I declared I would be a writer, Mom cheering me on as first reader and reviewer. These creative outlets would become necessary coping mechanisms as, by age eleven, I experienced firsthand loss, grief, uncertainty, cruelty, frailty, courage, and perseverance. A truncated childhood gained the weight of adult responsibilities made bearable only with art. My most troubling issues became a springboard into poetry.

My chapbook, *Splintered Memories*, explores my late mother's debilitating illnesses—mental and physiological—and our complicated bond. With time came healing; my subjects broadened as I found my voice. Today, diverse interests fuel my creativity, among them, environmental conservation, sustainability, peace, egalitarianism, animal welfare, sustenance, the arts, and architecture. My photographer's eye focuses on detail, form, color, and texture, informing my poetry. Years of music study inspired the infusion of sound into my writing. By translating personal or witnessed struggle or triumph into image-rich, relatable vignettes, I strive to offer readers a tactile sensory experience. Accessibility is a constant goal.

I've written of family and friendship dynamics, caregiving, abandonment, estrangement, loss of memory and mobility, and death, as well as joy, humor, empathy, and discovery. Poetry rescued me. This isn't hyperbole—I find poetry a life-affirming, satisfying means of owning my purpose and connecting meaningfully with others. I rely on poetry to soothe unchecked angst in the moment, comfort lingering despair.

I further use poetry to question what fails to serve societal good and our planet's health. My ecopoetry is informed by an ache to understand humankind's self-serving relationship with Mother Nature and other life on this fragile earth. We who commit to living gently and responsibly are at the mercy of those whose willful abuse of resources stems from greed. I believe all life is inextricably connected, lament others' denial of accountability.

It took me decades to take myself less seriously. Rupracht rhymes with roof rack, sumac, and Muzak. I've written that poem, too.

Whose Bone This Winter Found

—After an untitled photograph by DJ Gaskin

*Every blade in the field, every leaf in the forest,
lays down its life in its season as beautifully as
it was taken up.* —Henry David Thoreau

Measured long as her house key
this fraction of a life passed
now fits in its finder's palm
turned over and again
its varied curves and textures
traced respectfully by curious
thumb and fingerprints

Unknown what animal
once carried
or was carried by
this composite of collagen
and calcium and miles journeyed
between flexing muscles
and elastic tendon freedom

Visualize where flesh
once connected
with nerves intertwined
for the art and science of movement
and now
in the absence of life
a sculpture remains

Imagine what creature
fled from predator's pursuit
betrayed by escape
or just lay down with gentle purpose

its tired body in tall creek-side grass
exhaled a last able breath
simply because

it was time

Passing Through

Child we'll never hold
steps over threshold toward the light

of ever-shine, the door closing behind her
a forever barrier between us and maybes

and promises buried deep in Carolina red clay.
Secret reasons float upon feathers, always

beyond our reach. Guardian pines whisper
her name to verdant moss blanketing her

long sleep. Grief's burden lighter with time,
may we forget to measure our breathing.

When the Rice Is Gone

—for Chuck

The gallon-sized bags you filled with
fragrant Basmati & gave me last fall

are down to three final cups. I've found
it's easier to count kindness in countless

tiny grains than tally the days since you
passed, or the days your friends & soul mate

must go without. I resist further depleting
this treasured supply cup by cup by cup

until nothing but the memory of your
generous heart remains.

CITY OF LONELY, LOST GLOVES

—for Will, who left a glove in an NYC taxicab

Whose hand wore this slender yellow knit before it fell
curbside on West 54th, drowned in thick, blackened slush?

Or that XL thermal fleece, abandoned on a barricade in
crowded Times Square, empty fingers pointing tourists

this way to Macy's, *that way* to where the sparkling ball
drops each New Year's Eve? In four days walking

Manhattan, I spy several one-offs, varied one from the next
by designer label or sidewalk vendor's cheap knockoff,

those that might not be missed from one's winter wardrobe.
Unless, of course, temps plunge to sub-freezing, air biting

as snow gently but steadily falls. I muse my observations to
my husband, ponder déjà vu, if we're walking in circles.

Quiet observer, he explains, *People remove a glove to text
on their smartphones,* then lose their loosed glove, lost

in digital distraction. Was that text even worth orphaning
the other hand's warmer? What becomes of all these

uncoupled gloves? Are they rounded up for disposal or
up-cycle? Do wayward mittens fall wayside as well?

I picture sewing found gloves into one-of-a-kind blankets
for the homeless, wrapping them in the caress of strangers

whose touch they might otherwise never know.

Lethal Food Chain

Moans rising from ocean depths, ghosts
haunt the tireless guardians who study garbage
exhumed from bellies of beached whales. Work
swiftly against fleeting minutes to untangle

commercial fishing nets and lines that bind sea turtle
flippers and shells, restrain plover and pelican wings,
obstruct lungs of dolphins. Sea lions. Seals. Manatees.

Some unlucky souls die ingesting toxic debris—
plastic bags, bottles, batteries, balloons. Polluted
bodies decay, or feed other innocents of the sea, heirs
to swallowed synthetics that never degrade.

Still more saltwater dwellers eat poison prey, survive
long enough for the contagion of willfull indifference
to swim full circle—

cedar plank grilled and served on a platter
with lemon, butter, a sprig of parsley, and a tangy
chutney of mango, mercury and microplastics.
Bon appétit.

Dying in the Dead of Winter

It's a terrible idea in Central New York's blizzard belt
where ground is unbreakable and well-hidden beneath
white stuff four feet deep and amassing. Damn it, Mom,

you've really put our family's lives on hold, while held
safe in the vault—maybe on ice, formaldehyde-fresh,
or already decaying—you don't realize we wait
to bury you. Closure seems impossible.

We wait some more—perhaps all we do now—
as hard earth concedes to another mid-spring snow,
soil eager for saturation with the season's last melt

so shovel, pick, and backhoe can ready the hole
into which your body, dressed in pink, black,
and white mother-of-the-bride outfit, will
heave one last time with the weight of

that heavy maple box, settle at six feet,
cocoon with cool earth, forever and further
still from our reach.

Diana Woodcock

Writing poetry is my way of bearing witness – of giving a voice to those who have no voice. It is how I promote worldwide justice and caretaking of the earth. It is how I pray, make sense of the world, rejoice and grieve. My poems arise from both a spiritual and an intellectual hunger, and from the questions I ponder about both the seen and unseen worlds. When my debut collection won the Vernice Quebodeaux International Poetry Prize for Women, it marked me as a poet of witness. By then, I had worked for nearly eight years in Tibet, Macau and in refugee camps on the Thai/Cambodian border.

Environmental issues and the role poetry plays in educating people about these issues have interested me for a very long time. Many of my published poems may be labeled ecopoetry. My most recently published full-length collection addresses the urgent issue of climate change. My second and third collections promote caretaking of not only a tiny oil-rich sheikdom at the edge of the Arabian Desert, but of the whole earth. My seventh chapbook was inspired by a recent Arctic Circle expedition. The research I conducted there is part of an ongoing project of writing ecopoems to shed light on endangered species and ecosystems. My sixth chapbook was inspired by a one-month residency (AIRIE/National Park Service) in the Everglades National Park. My fifth focuses on the endangered flora of the Arabian Desert.

British poet Helen Farish, in her endorsement of my chapbook, Tamed by the Desert, wrote that my poetry is "reminiscent of Amy Clampitt in its scholarly attention to detail and its rigorous insistence on linguistic precision." It has been described as a cross between photography and painting – each poem as sharply focused and true to life as a photograph, yet with a touch of impressionism and painting en plein air, like Monet's Sunrise – capturing the momentary and transient effects of elements of the natural world. Some poems read like documentaries (but with a lyrical rhythm), providing historical vignettes of past and present dramas that have played out on Earth's stage.

STREAKED-WINGED RED SKIMMER

One dragonfly lingers
on the brown tip of a summer
green reed like a flame
on a candle at mass.

Poison has spoiled its meal
of midges and broken its eggs.
The last of its kind
to inhabit this shoreline,

it hangs on,
burns in the mid-day sun,
purifying the day.
No longer skimming

its lake, it poses on its reedy
throne—a lone ember
glowing in the fumes
of Malathion.

I Could Become the Phoenix

For the wild thorns grow tame
And will do nothing to oppose the flame . . .
~ Robert Lowell

I could become volatile and travel
on the air—become a thistle seed whisked
away by my bristly parachute of long
white hairs—if I would just stop clinging
to the earth.

I could laze all day:
a vine snake posing as a branch,
trading my culinary concerns
for a lucky chance at sustenance,
if I would simply accept whatever
comes within reach.

I could become the phoenix, or
at the very least wild thorns not
resisting the flame—not grasping,
not clinging. I could scintillate till
I finally ignite—phoenix-like—
from nothing more or less than
midnight tears' heat.

Cupful of Light

Here, let me pour light into this cup
and raise it to your parched heart,
as Hafiz did for me. Then come, let's go
together to Salsabeel, that spring in Paradise—
leave behind the noise, even jazz-metal fusion.
We'll keep a night-watch for fluxion
and phantoms of past and future—
strive to forget selves, remember God.

Come, let's sit here facing the suhaili wind,
sleep under the white sheet light
of the moon, cling neither to *gold
and jewels nor tile and pebble.**

Let's expand with hope till we *leave off
the two worlds in one rapture to cast
[ourselves] on a hundred new worlds.***
Let's stretch toward heaven, become all
flame—desert father Joseph said *Make this
your aim* as he lit up the sky
with his ten fingers of fire.

Come stand still with me and listen,
inhale, feel, touch all in silence
and gratitude for Ghebayra,***
suhaili, bulbul and Broad-billed
sandpiper, camel and gazelle,
desert and swale, seif and barchan dunes,
Spiny-tailed agamas and Sand vipers.

Come sit with me under the sidra tree.
Let's begin afresh like the budding branches,

lay aside our wrathful grapes, realize how
fragile are all the vagile organisms
surrounding and sustaining us.

  *Dogen
 **Fariduddin 'Attar
***Herniaria hemistemon

Called Out by Bulbuls

There are hundreds of ways to kneel and kiss the ground.
~ Rumi

Today I found yet another way
to kneel and pray – set out
a shallow pan filled with water,
a bird-bath for the bulbuls.

Got quiet and still,
shut out the unbearable world
to be at home with white-eared softbills,
Pycnonotus leucotis, those precocious

socialites. Together we praised
the silent earth, her dark loam,
mold and sod, dust and dew.
I learned from the bulbuls to do

nothing but sit and sway
on a branch of bougainvillea all day,
just being. Doing nothing,
yet nothing left undone.*

Abstained from weeding, the heart bleeding
for the most common green shoot.
Quiet and still, just sitting and being,
considering how the politics of speed

deprives us of our natural habitats.
This little coastal town turned
upside down, thanks to oil and gas,
air and water pollution.

I sat and meditated, the solution
not so far-fetched – escape the blind
process of proliferation –
participation in third-world

exploitation and pollution.
In solitude and solidarity
with bulbuls, a clarity,
a sense of finitude overwhelms one.

The bulbuls call like chimes
to one another – a sound-map of this
desert town, songline from aridity to sea.
No mountains and moors,

nothing here but low desert terrain,
dunes shifting toward the sea (a saline
body on three sides of me),
and the miswak tree – fruit

upon which bulbuls love to gorge.
The urgency of Carson's silent spring
surrounds me – everything but the bulbuls
and palm doves gone silent.

Holding still, folding into leafy shade,
I – like the bulbuls – fill myself again
with the breath of leaves,
all that sustains me.

*from the *Tao Te Ching*

Facing Aridity

*Do not divert your love from visible things. But go on loving what is good,
simple and ordinary – animals and flowers, and keep the balance true.*
— Rainer Maria Rilke

Home again, I unpack the sounds,
close my eyes and listen till I'm back
among anhingas, little green and cricket
frogs, bellowing alligators, a thunderstorm.

First one set aside to preserve biological
(not geological) resources, it'll flow now
through my veins like honey, like
streams in a desert—in this dot of a desert,

finger pointing into the Arabian Sea.
Everglades nourishing me as it does
wading birds in the sawgrass sea,
fresh water meandering southward

toward Florida Bay.
Back among Islamic mosaics,
I now treasure another kind: of
ponds and sloughs, hardwood

hammocks, sawgrass marshes –
fragile wetlands for endangered
manatee, Wood stork, Florida panther,
Cape Sable seaside sparrow.

Thunder peals as ibis, herons,
spoonbills spill over Eco Pond.
Subtropical wonderland sounds
to refresh my withering soul.

National treasure, delicate ecosystem of unsurpassable diversity, help me face aridity and keep the balance true.

Learning to Tread Softly

To learn how to tread softly,
take counsel of the Bridled tern
on the open sea, resting
on any floating piece of debris
that's drifted its way.

Taking your heaviness away,
it'll make you light as one of its white
underwing feathers as it urges you
to merge with the salty air till you could
swear your body has disappeared.

Or observe the Swift tern
on an offshore island
laying its single egg
right onto the holy sand –
no need of a nest.

The lighter we tread,
the more we absorb
of earth's holiness –
each patiently soft footfall
giving birth to the fragile earth.

Explorations of evolutions,
geological holiness, fullness
and transience of Earth's wonders.
Holy ground trembling under
the weight of human mistakes –

whole landscapes laid to waste
by those who never learned to tread softly.
The secret is to feel the cord
binding you to the earth – to terns gracing
islands and coasts of the Red Sea,

Arabian Gulf. Never trudging,
always treading softly – believing
all of it is holy – even, especially,
when ravished by locusts, malaria-
carrying mosquitos, chlorpyrifos clouds.

Feet touching nothing as you levitate.
But wait – that isn't the goal,
to rise above it all. No, no, no.
You're missing the point.
Come back down to earth.

For what it's worth,
divinity can wait. Tread softly
among side-winding snakes and
desert rodents – gerbils, jirds, jerboas
who have nowhere else to go.

Feel every tendril and vein tingle
with intoxication of softly treading
over Aeolian sands – hummock
and barchan dunes, rocky hamadas,
wadis and runnels,

dune fields of coalesced barchans,
marine coastal sands of quartz.
All of it holy, holy, holy.
Tread softly, let the body –
merging with salt and air – disappear.

Publication Credits

Sharon Alexander

"Blood Season" originally appeared in Sharon Alexander's first chapbook, VOODOO TROMBONE (Finishing Line Press, 2014), and subsequently in her second chapbook, INSTRUCTIONS IN MY ABSENCE (Palettes & Quills, 2017).

"In the Half-Light of the Forest" originally appeared in Idyllwild Life Magazine (Spring - Summer 2020), in a slightly different incarnation under the title "Another Kind of Birdsong".

Margo Berdeshevsky

Between Tree And Rocket: (previously published in Plume poetry journal)

One Answer, Or None To Hers or His or Mine (previously published in Harbor Review)

Bridge In The City Of Light   (previously published in Cimarron Review)

Marcene Gandolfo

December Magazine: "Cleave," "Exit"

Glass: A Journal of Poetry: "When She Leaves, I Think of Demeter in Autumn"

Fifth Wednesday Journal: "Circle with Two Lines from Job"

Rappahannock Review: "Lorca's Guitar"

Brad Rose

"Cotton-Candy Pink," "Like and Accident," and "Long Black Car," appeared in The American Journal of Poetry.

"Suburban Landscape (with Flying Saucer)" appeared in appeared in Sequestrum.

"It All Depends" appeared in concis.

"Windows" appeared in streetcake.

Leslie M. Rupracht

KAKALAK 2014 Carolina Poetry and Art, Main Street Rag Publishing, Beth Ann Cagle, Lisa Zerkle, and Richard Allen Taylor, editors: "Whose Bone This Winter Found"

K'in, Issue 8, Nov. 2021 (www.kinliteraryjournal.com), Mary Carroll-Hackett, editor-at-large, Semein Washington and Thomas Dixon, poetry editors: "When the Rice Is Gone"

Diana Woodcock

"Streak-winged Red Skimmer"— *Least-loved Beasts of the Really Wild West*, Native West Press (anthology, Spring 1997); Creekwalker, Summer 2007; Swaying on the Elephant's Shoulders (Little Red Tree Publishing), 2011; Canary, Summer 2014 (Issue 25)

"I Could Become the Phoenix"— *Homestead Review*, Spring/Summer 2004 (No. 20, Issue 2); *Swaying on the Elephant's Shoulders* (Little Red Tree Publishing), 2011

"Cupful of Light"– International Honor Scroll/Senior Poets Laureate, 2009 http://www.amykitchenerfdn.org/international_09/qatar.html; *In the Shade of the Sidra Tree* (chapbook), 2010; *Under the Spell of a Persian Nightingale* (Word Poetry/WordTech Communications), 2015

"Called Out by Bulbuls"– *Raven Chronicles*, Summer 2017 (Vol. 24, HOME issue)

"Facing Aridity"— *Convergence: an online journal of poetry and art*, Spring 2011 http://www.convergence-journal.com/summer11/su11p2.html#Woodcock

"Beggar in the Everglades" (Finishing Line Press), 2016; *Facing Aridity* (Homebound Publications/Wayfarer Press), 2021

"Learning to Tread Softly"– *Written River: A Journal of Eco-Poetics*, 2016 (Issue 10); *Tread Softly* (FutureCycle Press), 2018

Contributor Notes

A native New Yorker, **Sharon Alexander** subsequently lived in California for many decades. She moved from Idyllwild, California to Benissa, Spain, in January 2020, six weeks before the nationwide Covid-19 lockdown. She now lives close to the Mediterranean with her husband and her husky, Bella.

Sharon was nominated for the Pushcart Prize by Moonrise Press in 2021. Her chapbook, *Instructions In My Absence*, won first place in the Palettes & Quills Chapbook Contest and was published in 2017. *Voodoo Trombone*, Sharon's previous chapbook, was published by Finishing Line Press in 2014.

Her poetry appears in numerous journals and on-line sites including *Barbaric Yawp*, *Caliban On-line*, *Idyllwild Life Magazine*, *Naugatuck River Review*, *Pinyon*, *Redheaded Stepchild*, *Santa Ana River Review*, *Slipstream*, *Subprimal*, and *Tiger's Eye*.

You can also find her work in the following anthologies: *Beyond the Lyric Moment* (Tebot Bach, 2014), *In the News* (The Poetry Box, 2018), *Poeming Pigeons* (The Poetry Box, 2015), *Spectrum: 140 SoCal Poets* (Don Kingfisher Campbell, 2015), *Village Poets Anthology* (Moonrise Press, 2020), and *Woman In Metaphor* (NHH Press, 2013).

Sharon's website is: *sharonalexanderpoetry.com*

Margo Berdeshevsky, born in New York city, often lives and writes in Paris. Her latest collection, *"Before The Drought,"* is from Glass Lyre Press, (a finalist for the National Poetry Series.) A new collection, *"It Is Still Beautiful To Hear The Heart Beat"* is forthcoming from Salmon Poetry. *"Kneel Said the Night (a hybrid book in half-notes)"* is forthcoming from Sundress Publications. Berdeshevsky is author as well of *"Between Soul & Stone,"* and *"But a Passage in Wilderness,"* (Sheep Meadow Press.) Her book of illustrated stories, *"Beautiful Soon Enough,"* received the first Ronald Sukenick Innovative Fiction Award for Fiction Collective Two (University of Alabama Press.) Other honors include the Robert H. Winner Award from the Poetry Society of America. Her works appear in

Poetry International, New Letters, The Night Heron Barks, Psaltry & Lyre, Kenyon Review, Plume, Scoundrel Time, The Collagist, Tupelo Quarterly, Gulf Coast, Southern Humanities Review, Pleiades, Prairie Schooner, The American Journal of Poetry, Jacar—One, Mānoa, Pirene's Fountain, Big Other, Dark Matter: Women Witnessing, among many others. In Europe and the UK her works have been seen in *The Poetry Review, PN Review, The Wolf, Europe, Siècle 21, Confluences Poétiques, Recours au Poème, Levure Littéraire, Under the Radar.* She may be found reading from her books in London, Paris, New York City, Los Angeles, Honolulu, at literary festivals, and/ or somewhere new in the world. Her "Letters from Paris" have appeared for many years in Poetry International online. Here is one: https://www.poetryinternationalonline.com/letter-from-paris-in-march-2019-from-margo-berdeshevsky/ For more information, kindly see here : http://margoberdeshevsky.com

Susan Michele Coronel's poems have appeared in numerous publications including Spillway 29, TAB Journal, The Inflectionist Review, The Ekphrastic Review, Gyroscope Review, Prometheus Dreaming, Redivider, and One Art. In 2021 one of her poems was runner-up for the Beacon Street Poetry Prize and another was a finalist for the Millennium Writing Award. In the same year, she received a Pushcart nomination and was longlisted for the Sappho Prize. She just completed her first full-length poetry manuscript, which was recently named a finalist for Harbor Editions' Laureate Prize.

Susan has a M.S. Ed. in Applied Linguistics from the City University of New York, and a B.A. in English from Indiana University-Bloomington, where she discovered the magic of writing poetry. Susan lives in New York City, where she owns and directs a preschool, and finds inspiration visiting art exhibits throughout the city. She is currently collaborating on a project with a flutist/composer, who is writing music to accompany Susan's poetry. The project will culminate in a public program that celebrates the diversity of Queens and the life of a late friend who devoted her life to teaching special needs children.

Marcene Gandolfo's poems have been published widely in literary journals, including *Poet Lore, Bellingham Review, december,* and *RHINO*. In 2014, her debut book, *Angles of Departure,* won *Foreword Reviews'* Silver Award for Poetry. She has taught writing and literature at several northern California colleges and universities. Marcene is currently a PhD candidate in Comparative Mythology at Pacifica Graduate Institute. Her dissertation explores mythological resonances in the poems of Brigit Pegeen Kelly.

Nicole Greaves holds an MFA from Columbia University and an MEd from Chestnut Hill College. Her poetry has appeared in numerous literary reviews and was awarded prizes by the Academy of American Poets and the Leeway Foundation of Philadelphia. She was a 2015 finalist for the Coniston Prize of *Radar Poetry,* who also nominated her for Best of the Net.

In 2020, she was a finalist for the Frontier Digital Chapbook Contest and the Dogfish Head Poetry Contest. Nicole is Poet Laureate Emeritus of Montgomery County, Pennsylvania, and she currently teaches English and creative writing in Philadelphia. She is also an academic coach. Nicole's mother came to the US from Panama at seventeen, and together they lived a life on the margins. Much of her work explores themes relating to this experience, specifically the tensions around acculturation, gender roles, and class. Her book, *Having Witnessed the Illusion,* is forthcoming in the spring/summer of 2022, from Glass Lyre Press. Find her at nicolegreaves.com

Raewyn Kraybill is a poet, college student, and loving but neglectful plant parent. Raewyn is currently attending Chatham University in Pittsburgh for Creative Writing.

Brad Rose was born and raised in Los Angeles, and lives in Boston. He is the author of three collections of poetry and flash fiction, *Pink X-Ray, de/tonations, and Momentary* Turbulence. Two new books of prose poems, *WordinEdgeWise* and *No. Wait. I Can Explain.*, are forthcoming, in 2022. Six times nominated for a Pushcart Prize, and three times nominated for the Best of the Net Anthology. Brad's poetry and fiction have appeared in, *The Los Angeles Times, The American Journal of Poetry, New York Quarterly, Puerto del Sol, Clockhouse, Cloudbank, Baltimore Review, Best Microfiction 2019, Lunch Ticket, Cultural Daily*, and other publications. Brad is also the author of seven poetry chapbooks, including the recently released *Collateral*, and *Funny You Should Ask*. His website is: www.bradrosepoetry.com

Lindsey Royce's poems have appeared in periodicals and anthologies, including the *Aeolian Harp #8, #7, and #5* anthologies; *Cutthroat: A Journal of the Arts* (periodicals and anthologies); *The Hampton-Sydney Review; The New York Quarterly, Poet Lore*, and *The Washington Square Review*. Her poems have been nominated for Pushcart Prizes in 2019, 2020, and 2021. Royce's first poetry collection, *Bare Hands*, was published by Turning Point in September of 2016, and her second collection, *Play Me a Revolution*, published by Press 53 in September of 2019, won second place for poetry in the 2020 Independent Publishers Book Awards.

Leslie M. Rupracht is an editor, poet, writer, and visual artist. Her poems appear in *Asheville Poetry Review, Gargoyle, Chiron Review, K'in, The Ekphrastic Review, Anti-Heroin Chic, As It Ought To Be, Kakalak, Poetry in Plain Sight, Kentucky Review, Main Street Rag*, and elsewhere. Nominated for *2020 Best of the Net*, Leslie also received honors in *Kakalak* and Charlotte Writers Club contests. Her chapbook is *Splintered Memories* (Main Street Rag Publishing). She earned her BA in English, minoring in studio art and public relations, at the State University of New York at Geneseo. Graduate work at Syracuse University focused on magazine editing. By day, Leslie spent nearly three decades in corporate and non-profit work. By night, she was the longtime senior associate editor of *Iodine*

Poetry Journal, prose and photography editor for *moonShine review*, and editor and designer of North Carolina Poetry Society's *Pinesong* anthology. Originally from Long Island and Central New York, Leslie transplanted to Charlotte, NC in 1997. She and her husband Will Weaver serve at the pleasure of their sweet rescued pit bull. Leslie produces and hosts *Waterbean Poetry Night at the Mic*, a monthly reading series she cofounded in 2015, at Waterbean Coffee in Huntersville, NC.

Diana Woodcock is the author of four full-length poetry collections: *Facing Aridity* (published in 2021 as a 2020 Prism Prize for Climate Literature finalist, Homebound Publications/Wayfarer Books), *Tread Softly*, *Under the Spell of a Persian Nightingale*, and *Swaying on the Elephant's Shoulders* (winner of the 2011 Vernice Quebodeaux International Women's Poetry Prize). Her seventh chapbook is *Near the Arctic Circle* (Tiger's Eye Press). Forthcoming in 2023 is *Holy Sparks* (a 2020 Paraclete Press Poetry Award finalist). A Pushcart Prize and Best of the Net nominee, she has had poems published in *Best New Poets 2008*, *Women's Review of Books*, *Nimrod*, *Crab Orchard Review*, *Southern Humanities Review*, *Spiritus*, *Comstock Review*, and elsewhere. Her grand prize-winning poem, "Music as Scripture," was performed onstage in Lincoln Park, San Francisco by Natica Angilly's Poetic Dance Theater Company at Artists Embassy International's 21st Dancing Poetry Festival. She holds a PhD in Creative Writing from Lancaster University, where her research was an inquiry into the role of poetry in the search for an enviromental ethic. For nearly eight years, she worked in Tibet, Macau, and on the Thai-Cambodian border. Since 2004, she has been teaching creative writing, environmental literature and composition at VCUarts Qatar.

Glass Lyre Press

exceptional works to replenish the spirit

Glass Lyre Press is an independent literary publisher interested in technically accomplished, stylistically distinct, and original work. Glass Lyre seeks diverse writers that possess a dynamic aesthetic and an ability to emotionally and intellectually engage a wide audience of readers.

Glass Lyre's vision is to connect the world through language and art. We hope to expand the scope of poetry and short fiction for the general reader through exceptionally well-written books, which evoke emotion, provide insight, and resonate with the human spirit.

Poetry Collections
Poetry Chapbooks
Select Short & Flash Fiction
Anthologies

www.GlassLyrePress.com